Proposition at the Walk-In Infinity Chamber

poems by

Bobbie Lee Lovell

Finishing Line Press
Georgetown, Kentucky

Proposition at the Walk-In Infinity Chamber

Copyright © 2017 by Bobbie Lee Lovell
ISBN 978-1-63534-266-6 First Edition
All rights reserved under International and Pan-American Copyright Conventions.
No part of this book may be reproduced in any manner whatsoever without written permission from the publisher, except in the case of brief quotations embodied in critical articles and reviews.

ACKNOWLEDGMENTS

The author gratefully acknowledges the editors of the publications in which the following poems first appeared, sometimes in slightly different versions:

Blue Heron Review • "Prayer at a Cliff's Edge" and "The Healing"
Bramble • "The Proposal"
Fox Cry Review • "The Divorcée"
Star*Line • "Mothership"
Verse-Virtual • "At the summit"
Wisconsin Poets' Calendar 2016 • "DST"
Wisconsin Poets' Calendar 2017 • "I Am River"

Additionally, "Mothership" received a Pushcart Prize nomination from *Star*Line*. "Every Day is a Close Call" was a 2014 Mill Poetry Prize honoree.

Publisher: Leah Maines

Editor: Christen Kincaid

Cover Art: iStock.com/m-gucci, Bobbie Lee Lovell

Author Photo: Bobbie Lee Lovell

Cover Design: Bobbie Lee Lovell

Printed in the USA on acid-free paper.
Order online: www.finishinglinepress.com
also available on amazon.com

Author inquiries and mail orders:
Finishing Line Press
P. O. Box 1626
Georgetown, Kentucky 40324
U. S. A.

Table of Contents

Proposition at the *Walk-In Infinity Chamber* 1
Singularity 2
The Proposal 3
Redheaded Stepchild 4
When to Say When? 5
I Am River 6
Dear Cinderella 7
Pachydermal Disparity 8
First Thought Upon Waking 9
How to Walk at Night in Suburbia 10
Last Time 11
Hotel Heart 12
The Divorcée 13
Prayer at a Cliff's Edge 14
The Healing 15
The Dance of Life 16
Youflower 18
Dismemberment 19
First Date 20
Riding with Aladdin 21
Window Seat 22
Camping with My (Single, Platonic) Friend 23
DST 25
Every Day Is a Close Call 26
What It Is About the Cliff 27
At the summit 28
Mothership 29

*With sincere gratitude to the arts community,
art appreciators and creatively-driven friends
for inspiring, welcoming and encouraging me—
sometimes indirectly and sometimes very directly.
You've made all the difference. ALL of it.*

Proposition at the *Walk-In Infinity Chamber*

Tonight, all the stars are aligned
in rows, like skyscraper windows.
Won't you cross the threshold with me?
Inside, we'll be human-shaped holes
in a caged galaxy. We'll be dark and sublime.
We'll be angels. Aliens. Explorers,
mapping the confines hand over hand
like mimes, then mapping each other,
swooning through space like two
of Chagall's lovers. Won't you have this
dance with me, here on the listing pseudo-
floor? It gets so hot—all that mirrored light—
so, stripped to bare essential, we'll dive
deep into the candle-studded sea, down,
down, or is it up, or everywhere at once,
like god? They say it's just an illusion,
but let's take our chances. Tomorrow
they'll find only hand prints, a smear
of goo on the glass, a lingering scent
that makes the *Janitor* blush. But tonight—
tonight we'll be the center of the universe.

Walk-In Infinity Chamber *(1968) is an installation by Stanley Landsman.*
Janitor *(1973) is a Hyperrealist sculpture by Duane Hanson.*
Both belong to the Milwaukee Art Museum's collection.

Singularity

> *I want to be inside your darkest everything.*
> —Frida Kahlo

I want to get lost

in your eyes, yes,
but more precisely
the pupils, those portals
that let in the light;

in the junctions and creases
where shadows huddle
to dream and scheme;

in the pit of your gut
with all the burnt-out stars
you've swallowed.

Forget the pristine pool,
the clear-to-the-bottom.
Bring on the unknown
                      depth.
I want to fall, not fathoms
but parsecs.

I want to jump,
for you to push
            (me)
I want   in.
to gasp/twitch/clench/slide

across your event horizon
where winning
is losing/is everything,

the pull so profound
not even light wants out.

The Proposal

It certainly wasn't about the ring.
My finger never felt naked,
bereft of the rock that baits others.

The proposal itself dazzled me,
the way the words hung in the air
like a little rainbow.

My parents would sigh with relief.
At last, a conventional path
for their black sheep daughter:

A wedding, a house, cute tiffs
about dinner and the toilet seat—
and grandchildren, of course.

He genuflected in our rented kitchen,
suds still dripping from dishpan hands,
and eyes aglow with hope.

It was about the electric silence
between the question
and the answer.

I wanted to cup his words
like magic beans in my hands
and never plant them.

But a person has to say something.
And with so much transforming power
cast out there, who wouldn't

be tempted to swallow
the exquisite fallacy
of two becoming one?

Redheaded Stepchild

The girl was ginger as sin. Dame Gothel
banked on Orphan Annie's sunshine
but wound up with sullen Rapunzel—
fetally swapped for unlimited rampion
salad, then stashed in a room with a view
but no door. Every day, Rapunzel dreamed
of jumping, broadcast all she'd prostitute
for freedom, wove yarns of words
that surged from fertile follicles, then
tossed 'em out the window on demand.
One day she refused. Fuming, Gothel
cobbled a ladder of switches and canes,
gagged Rapunzel and wrapped her hands
to trap the words within until they
smothered. When the requisite prince
came a-knockin', Gothel said, "Take her!"
He called to Rapunzel, "Let down your
guard," and she did. He wagged his penis,
released her hands and promptly drowned
in a flood of suppressed expression. Now
she roams the forest, casting lines of poetry
like bait. She climbs the tallest tree and
reminisces, her hair a flag of warning.

When to Say When?

Never. Not when the first drop
pings against the bottom
of your empty cup
like prayed-for rain.
Not when the splatter gives way
to the slurping vortex.
Not when you're wavering between
half-empty and half-full,
not enough and too much.
Not when the level rises to the rim,
and you're calculating maximum volume
while recklessly anticipating the spill.
Not when it finally cascades over the edge
like a breached dam, first in rivulets, then sheets,
then shamelessly gushing.
Not as the puddle expands across the table
like an advancing war front.
Not when the first uncomfortable wetness
storms the beach of your lap
and spreads between your thighs
as though you've pissed yourself.
Not when it seeps beneath the door
like the first horrifying moment of truth
for *Titanic*'s passengers.
Not when the carpet is ruined and the furniture adrift.
Not when you're ankle-deep, knee-deep,
waist-deep, shoulder-deep. Not when you're in
way over your head. Not when everything
you once knew and loved is submerged,
not when all you see is an unbroken horizon
in every direction, not when you're forced to choose
between sinking or swimming, and not even
when you're drowning. Never.

I Am River

I am a reckless nomad born on high.
I heed the call of sea and gravity.
I leap from cliffs in splendid arcs of foam,
then pool and swirl but always must proceed.
I am already where I'll be next week
and am still where I traveled yesterday.
I circumvent whatever I can't float.
I laugh at all that dares to block my way.
You dam me, damn me, try to make me lake,
but I am river and will not be still.
Even if my surface freezes hard,
beneath, my current won't accept your will.
Along to greater things I'm bound to flow.
I never doubt there is somewhere to go.

Dear Cinderella

Go to hell. Get off your high horse,
if that's even *your* horse, or a horse at all.

You and your rags-to-riches rubbish,
spewing rainbows where sun won't shine,
how many maidens, wistful and oppressed,
have you duped into compliance
with your gospel of karma?

Any fairy godmother of mine
better have more up her sleeve
than a fancy dress and a wayward shoe.
Girl, you might as well have been
conked by a rock, dragged off by your hair.

After happily ever after,
when Charming no longer muffles his farts,
someone must still clean the toilets.
And, Highness, your crib has a lot of 'em.

I would know, wouldn't I? Look around:
The world is full of cinder girls clinging to hope,
yet your tale grants *one* godmother. *One* prince.

So, you're hardly the poster girl
for dreams come true. Make your own magic—
then I'll be impressed.

Pachydermal Disparity

"There's a giant, silent elephant in the room,"
you say, and watch for my reaction.
Perhaps I should be affected, but instead

I've conjured *The Elephant Celebes*,
fixed on that colossal Weber grill,
its dislocated tusks and metaphysical toys.

Could your anger fill such volume, rush through
that vacuum-hose proboscis like a mammoth fart,
cause planes to fall from the sky?

Perhaps, but I'm more concerned with recalling
the artist: "Max Ernst!" Now it's pink and dancing.
Now there's a herd, and I'm queen.

You raise an eyebrow, then sigh.
You realize you've already lost me,
that the creature has swallowed me whole.

The Elephant Celebes *(1921) is a Surrealist painting featuring a giant mechanical elephant.*

First Thought Upon Waking

Sometimes it's relief
that the dream was a dream—
for not falling to certain death,
for teeth still rooted in place,
for not even once
forgetting to dress.

Sometimes it's praise
for silence—no sirens,
no summons, no storm after all.
Sometimes it's roll call:
Who, What, Where and *When*.
(*Why* and *How* are tardy.)

Sometimes it's the burning
urgency of my bladder.
Or how the woosh of the train
sounds so unlike
the moaning locomotives
that rattled my childhood home.

Sometimes it's just:
Oh, crap. The light. Or disdain
for a shallow songster
on the old clock radio. For a time
it was that the towers had fallen.
And once: *What if it's cancer?*

Today it's that you're leaving,
and I want to close my eyes
like Princess Aurora
until you hack your way back
through the brambles
and finally set things right.

How to Walk at Night in Suburbia

You don't need a flashlight. It's never as dark as you think. Besides, there are stars and streetlights. Every so often, you'll snuff one with your mind. The kids say streetlights are Santa's surveillance cameras ... or maybe Batman's. You never know. See how the light falls in ombré cones? See the swarming moths? Each bulb is a moon they never expected to reach. You are neither moth nor light—you just *are*. You, too, will know the moon. You'll learn where it rises and sets, which phases cast your shadow. Address it as you wish, but don't expect it to answer you. You'll learn, also, the name of any dog let out during the wee hours. Watch for turds and toads. Watch for Ted, who also walks at night and *will* answer you. If you think you've seen a meteor, or a UFO, or a ghost, or the bogeyman, or Ted—you have. Between streetlights, you can disappear. When you return home, understand you've gone much farther than your feet have taken you. See, it's never as dark as you think. Sometimes it's darker.

Last Time

Last time, you broke and entered
like a thief, but tonight you knock
softly, as though I've upgraded
to a library filled with wisdom,
or a church brimming with belief.
I'm loath to entertain guests,
the linens and dinnerware packed,
this place more warehouse than home.
I can't afford the mortgage
                              anymore.
I'm almost bankrupt already. Still,
I confess how I changed the lock,
how solid the door's always been.

Then I let you in, and we feast
on all that remains, the flavors
sorely craved, divinely amplified.
Sparks sweep from closet
to salon, ignite a retrospective
of Abstract Expressionism—
first, bleeding around the edges
like a Rothko, then building
to the manic grandeur of a Pollack.

Bare walls re-dressed, I long to stay.
But it's all in my head. You can't
see this. Perhaps I shouldn't either,
but oh, you knocked so softly.

Hotel Heart

There's never *No Vacancy*.
It's bigger inside than out,
a sprawling mansion
of cavelike spaces
with stalactites like uvulae.

Some guests become
permanent residents
whether they know it or not.
Others are transient,
on business or pleasure
or seeking safe haven.

Sometimes it's simpler
to seal a room shut
than to clean up
the mess left behind.
A person can always add on.

The Divorcée

She paid the price.
Now silence pools in spaces
where impasse shrieked,
and every interaction
glistens with potential.

She dishes from greener grass
to jaded still-marrieds.
"When you aren't gettin' any,
you miss it," she quips.
They are incredulous: *"Really?"*

You'd think she'd claim the bed,
lie spread eagle
and flail with abandon,
not hunched on one side
hugging warmth to her core.

Sometimes she forgets,
the way you don't remember
growing older, slips
with a mindless reversion
of pronouns, a defunct *we*.

She watches a movie
of her choosing
and turns toward empty air,
itching to discuss the sudden
turn of plot, the foreseen ending.

But even *before*,
he wouldn't have been there.
And so, she grieves twice.

Prayer at a Cliff's Edge

Let me live like this tenacious tree.
Let me rise from the earth
like a skeletal hand from the grave,
reach boldly over the edge

for the sun, the stars,
the tantalizing unknown.
And when I grasp nothing but air,
let that be something. Let that be enough.

Let me flourish in hostile places,
my roots shallow, yet secure,
my surface scorched and scarred,
my soul no worse for the wear.

    And if I can't have peace,
    then let me have purpose.

Let the wind whistle and moan
the song of my shape. Let me be refuge
and music. Let my leaves whisper
summer love, then rattle frosty rhythms

until they're stripped away. Even then,
let me hold my ground, frozen in time
like a Boccioni bronze, resolved to bud
on the breath of spring, again and again.

The Healing

One day it happens.
The morning sun dazzles
rather than burns,
and the grass beneath your own feet
looks green enough.

You don't know how
you got here, and you don't
trust the healing.
Perhaps you've just found
a new way to cope,
to self-medicate.

But even numbness
feels different, and look:
where your wound gaped
wide as a primal scream,
a close-lipped scar now smiles.
My touch merely tingles.

Freedom feels so foreign
you reconsider the cage.
But that choice is no choice.
So you leap, and wings appear.
You fly into the dawn.

The Dance of Life
After The Dance of Life *(1900) by Edvard Munch*

Transfigured here
is Edvard's enigmatic other
split to a trinity of before/during/after
while his likeness appears
for the main event, as though
summoned by a dinner bell.

You might be put off
by this scene that suggests
woman is so incomplete without man
that even her hair, her dress
must conspire to ensnare him—
but it's not the dance of *love*.

The leftmost figure blushes
in virginal white, contemplating
deflowerment—carnal and literal—
in that pivotal moment before
anticipation blooms into experience,
then decays into memory.
Smiling sweetly, she reaches
toward temptation.

Her bitter alter ego, onyx-eyed
and stiff in her crow-colored gown,
wrings her hands so tightly
they've gone gangrenous. You know
she's got one foot in the grave,
her still-bright tresses trumped
by the scowl of utter regret:
the flower, once picked, cannot live.

The omniscient moon hovers
above its elongated reflection,
colossal pink cock teasing
the shoreline tableau. The moon
whispers, *It's a mindfuck.*
The flower would die anyway.

You've succumbed to the spell.
You desperately want to be
the passion-hued half of the rapt central pair
melding into her mate,
oblivious to the world in her enviable prime,
entranced in the bliss of *now*.

You are still the woman in red.
You are still dancing. You are, you are.
Well, aren't you?

Youflower

Severed helianthus
sips liquid optimism
in mason jar
on window sill, and still
believes in light.

Dismemberment

Your right hand
is splayed across
your denim-clad thigh
like a crouching tiger.

Its slender digits
have baited hooks,
keyed countless words,
tickled riffs from guitars,
coaxed orgasmic moans.

I study the elegant structure:
the scuffed knuckles,
the callused pads,
my whole being tuned
to the wondrous potential
of proximity.

We might never love
all of each other
all at once.
One part at a time.
It's safer this way.

First Date

In the quest for someone like you who isn't you,
I've done well. I eye him across a table for two:
goatee, glasses, black coat, black boots—
adorably nerdy with hints of a goth phase
long abandoned, fondly remembered.

Conversation flows, begets segue after segue
and all is delightfully well, yet it all
seems strangely distant and rippled.
He has much to say, and I realize I want this:
someone who never stops talking.

The waiter presumes we have history. Har!
I don't know whether he snores, if he likes it
rough, much less how he likes his coffee,
our canvas as clean as our plates. I've barely
dipped my toe into the murky lake of him.

Somehow, you're there, Fauvist and fluorescing,
your light outshining your dark so brightly I can't
look directly at it, nor completely away. It turns out
I'm gazing across the table from the floor
of an ocean I dove into years ago. I think he knows.

Riding with Aladdin

"Do you trust me?" he asks.
The question unsettles me.
No one trusts anyone anymore,
I want to say. Trust is cliché, obsolete.

He lacks a lamp but fancies me
his princess, dares me to deny
the romance of trusting
the kindly stranger, the thief.

He is waiting. "Of course," I say.

We are, after all, riding the same
sputtering rug. We've flown to the edge
of the world, and not once did I fear
he might elbow me off it.

"Good," he says, "because *I* trust *you*."

He smiles, and I am further disturbed
that he is appeased. I wish
I felt so certain. Where's a genie
when you need one?

Window Seat

Oh, to pirouette
careless on the wing, then fall
dizzy to the clouds.

Camping with My (Single, Platonic) Friend

Real flames dance between us.
We dream up provisions for love:
kinetic awareness, creative drive
and for godssake no clinging.
We pretend not to notice
we're making one list.

Any algorithm
would have matched us
long ago. Half the world
wonders; the other assumes.
But we're so above that,
won't have any of it,

no *When-Harry-Met-Sally* thing
transcending miles and years,
goodbyes and hellos—
no shining moment of truth
at this campsite tonight
among flirting fireflies.

A storm passes to the south,
gives a silent show of tangled bolts.
We feed the fire; it applauds
gratefully. Clouds break.
Every light source flickers on and off.
Words flow easy as breath.

Later, we leave the embers
to their own conclusions,
zip ourselves away
from the winking stars,
whisper good night and lie
separately cocooned,

so close I hear his breath
like a beacon beyond seeing,
infrared or ultraviolet.
We light each other's dreams
yet will not dare to cross
the line the burns between us.

DST

The solstice seemed
light years away.
We circled the wormhole,
danced around the rim
as close as we dared to get
to getting there, blinked
and paid the annual toll
at the stroke of two,
an hour we could afford
to lose. We had, after all,
declared ourselves still young,
still blessed with all the time
in the world—any world.
The night went on
unchecked 'til dawn
confirmed we'd lost nothing
in that dark hour
when we saved the light,
when we saved everything.

Every Day Is a Close Call

It's the blessed dry patch
on the icy road,
the averted collision,
the well-timed jerk awake
or slam of brakes,

the last-chance branch
cantilevered from the cliff,
the arm that shoots out
to break your fall,
the fluky fistful of fabric and hair,

the dropped knife that spares the foot,
the gun discharged sans bullet,
all the lightning that strikes
                              elsewhere,
the instinctive dodge,
the ducking,

the time you took the other route
for the hell of it, or stayed home,
the fortuitous sick day,
the lucky thwarted plan,

the word lodged in your throat,
the love-charged moment grounded
by shifted eyes, random distraction,

the narrow victory
of sage restraint

that keeps you safe.

What It Is About the Cliff

Each time I flee to the crumbling precipice,
leap the narrow chasm and wax
triumphant atop the limestone tower, each time
I plop my butt on the chilly rim and dangle my legs
above the trees, admire the sight of feet released
from the ground—each time, a choice presents itself,
however subconscious, however primal:
the urge to slide off the edge without fanfare,
or to run boldly as Icarus into the air, suspended
for a nanosecond before gravity says *Never*.
Each time, I leap back and re-shoulder the yoke
of worldly cares, its buckets heavy with bricks of loss
and duty. It's said that if we attempted
to barter our troubles, we'd take back our own,
the ones about which we know something.
Each time I return from the cliff is a Holy Yes
to living, to resilience.

At the summit

you find it was really
about the climb—
the trophy scrapes and bruises,
the tale of near disaster.
Nonetheless, you savor the view:
galaxies of pinpoint trees,
the sugar cube city,
silver veins of river.

Across the valley,
a grander peak gleams.
You nod your respects,
make a vow to return.
You know there will always be
another time, a greater height.
You know you were born
to die climbing—

not mountains, exactly.
They're just metaphors.

Mothership

When the silver saucer
finally returned, hovered
above the suburb and caught me
in its beam, I was afraid.

I never thought I'd balk,
feel anything but joy. I'd waited
so long. Pined nearly to death.
Yet homesickness waned

to complacence. I got comfy
in human skin, acquiesced
to the primitive patterns
of Earth years, earthling lives.

I fooled all, loved some,
built a family and flourished.
When my own kind came
calling at last, time froze,

all outcomes reduced to *stay* or *go*.
It had to be clean—no goodbye,
no reason. A simple disappearance,
an endless evening stroll.

In that shaft of light, two worlds
fused, then split again.
You know what happened next.
You would have done the same.

Bobbie Lee Lovell grew up writing, drawing and dreaming on Lake Michigan's western shore. She studied visual art and pursued a graphic communications career, but words are her favorite medium. Bobbie has worked as a magazine art director, a freelance graphic designer and a corporate print producer. Her poems have received honors via the *Peninsula Pulse*'s Hal Prize and the Wisconsin Fellowship of Poets' Muse and Triad contests. She won the 2016 Kay Saunders Memorial New Poet Award and has been a Pushcart Prize and Best of the Net nominee. This is her first chapbook.

Bobbie remains in Wisconsin with her two children and a vibrant poetry community. Her hiking shoes and camera get much use—often simultaneously.

www.ingramcontent.com/pod-product-compliance
Lightning Source LLC
LaVergne TN
LVHW041507070426
835507LV00012B/1401